Food for Life

ARCTIC TUNDRA

KATE RIGGS

D1511568

Published by Creative Paperbacks
P.O. Box 227, Mankato, Minnesota 56002
Creative Paperbacks is an imprint of The Creative Company
www.thecreativecompany.us

Design and production by Liddy Walseth
Art direction by Rita Marshall
Printed in Malaysia

Photographs by Alamy (Arco Images GmbH, Robert E. Barber,
BRUCE COLEMAN INC., Visual&Written SL, Jim Zuckerman), Corbis
(Richard Cummins), Getty Images (Altrendo Nature, Daniel J Cox, Michael
Durham, Charles Krebs, Roine Magnusson, John E Marriott, Paul Nicklen,
Michael S. Quinton, Paul Souders, Gary Vestal, Art Wolfe),
SuperStock (Roberta Olenick/All Canada Photos)

Library of Congress Cataloging-in-Publication Data
Riggs, Kate.
Arctic tundra / by Kate Riggs.
p. cm. — (Food for life)
Includes index.
Summary: A fundamental look at a common food chain on the arctic tundra,
starting with the low-growing arctic willow, ending with the arctic wolf, and
introducing various animals in between.
ISBN 978-1-58341-831-4 (hardcover)
ISBN 978-1-62832-105-0 (pbk)
1. Tundra ecology—Juvenile literature. 2. Food chains (Ecology)—
Juvenile literature.
I. Title. II. Series.

QH541.5.T8R54 2010
577.5'8616—dc22 2009004784

First Edition
2 4 6 8 9 7 5 3 1

Food for Life
ARCTIC TUNDRA

KATE RIGGS

A food chain shows what living things in an area eat. Plants are the first link on a food chain. Animals that eat plants or other animals make up the rest of the links.

POLAR BEARS ARE LARGE ARCTIC _PREDATORS_. THEY HUNT FOR SEALS ON THE ICE NEAR OPEN WATER.

The arctic (ARK-tick) tundra is a cold and dry place. It is close to the North Pole. The ground there stays mostly frozen year-round. But in the summer, plants grow up through the snow.

WOLVES AND BEARS EAT BIG
(KARE-ih-boo). CARIBOU EAT

DEER CALLED CARIBOU PLANTS SUCH AS LICHEN (LY-ken).

The arctic willow is a short plant. It has small, green leaves. The leaves are a good food source. They have _**nutrients**_ (NOO-tree-ents) that animals need.

Lemmings eat arctic willows. A lemming is a small _rodent_. It has thick, brown fur and sharp claws. It has to eat fresh food all the time. It does not store food like some animals do.

THE ARCTIC FOX EATS
SNOWY OWLS. IT EATS

BOTH LEMMINGS AND
ANY MEAT IT CAN FIND.

Ermines eat lemmings. Ermines are _mammals_. **They make their _dens_ near lemmings.** An ermine's fur changes from brown to white in the winter. Then it can hide in the snow.

Ermines cannot always hide from snowy owls. Snowy owls can see their _prey_ at night and hear them underground. The large owls fly quietly. They use their claws to catch ermines.

WOLVERINES ARE ARCTIC TUNDRA SCAVENGERS. THEY EAT THE LEFTOVERS OF DEAD ANIMALS.

Arctic wolves sometimes eat snowy owls. The owls make their nests on the ground. Arctic wolves can smell the owls' nests and hear baby owls from far away. The big wolves attack the nests.

All of these living things make up a food chain. The arctic willow grows on the tundra. The lemming eats the arctic willow. The ermine eats the lemming. The snowy owl eats the ermine. And the arctic wolf eats the snowy owl.

PLANT-EATING MUSK OXEN ANIMALS ON THE

ARE SOME OF THE BIGGEST
ARCTIC TUNDRA.

Some day, the arctic wolf will die. Its body will break down into nutrients. These nutrients will go into the ground and help plants such as the arctic willow grow. Then the arctic tundra food chain will start all over again.

READ MORE ABOUT IT

Fleisher, Paul. *Tundra Food Webs*. Minneapolis: Lerner Publications, 2008.

Kalman, Bobbie, and Kelley MacAulay. *Tundra Food Chains*. New York: Crabtree Publishing Company, 2006.

GLOSSARY

dens—wild animals' homes; they are sometimes underground

mammals—animals that have hair or fur and give birth to live young

nutrients—things in soil and food that help plants and animals grow strong and healthy

predators—animals that kill and eat other animals

prey—an animal that is killed and eaten by another animal

rodent—an animal such as a rat, mouse, or squirrel that has strong front teeth

INDEX

arctic foxes 12–13

arctic willows 10–11, 18, 23

arctic wolves 8, 17, 18, 23

caribou 8–9

ermines 14–15, 18

food chains 4, 18, 23

lemmings 11, 13, 14, 18

musk oxen 20–21

nutrients 10, 23

polar bears 6

scavengers 16

snowy owls 12, 15, 17, 18